THE RICA MODEL

...pathway to a fulfilling marriage

Sola & Nike Ajayi

Copyright © 2023

The rights of Sola & NIke Ajayi to be identified as the authors of this work has been asserted by them in accordance with the copyright laws.

All rights reserved.

No part of this publication may be reproduced, stored in a retrieval system or transmitted in any form or by any means, electronic, mechanical, photocopying, recording or otherwise without the prior permission of the author or publisher.

ISBN - 978-978-782-758-1

Published by:
Heart2World Publishing
Ago Palace Way. Lagos
w. heart2worldpublishing.org
t. 09056183960
e. heart2worldpublishing@gmail.com

Unless otherwise stated, scripture quotations are from The Holy Bible: King James Version. Cambridge, 1769. Used by permission. All rights reserved.

For information on distribution, translation or bulk sales, please contact:

Sola Ajayi
Phone:+2348023415303, 08023415645
Email: therealmtribe@gmail.com

Dedication

This book is dedicated to the One who gave humanity the gift of marriage, the Immortal, Invisible, and the Only wise God.

Acknowledgement

RICA acronym could not have become a reality without the contribution of Olalekan Adesina, popularly known as Elgee. I remember he anchored one of the interview sessions during the RCCG Convention, and I was invited to speak on relationships. He mentioned RICA after speaking on Revelation, Information, Comprehension, and Application. That stuck, and here we are with the book on RICA. Thank you, Elgee, for the unique inspiration.

Thank you, P. Daniel Olawande, for calling to ignite the confirmation that a book must be written on the RICA model.

We acknowledge the feedback from all the singles and couples we have been privileged to counsel on all six continents of the world. Thank you for trusting us with your lives and marriage.

We want to especially thank three couples out of many in particular whose marriages were already so bad and it seemed they were at points of no return. They had already signed in for divorce in court. Thank you for allowing God to breathe afresh into your marriage.

We appreciate in advance as many who will buy this book read through and use the added workbook to ignite their relationship and marriage. We celebrate you.

Foreword

Sola & Nike Ajayi are my colleagues in the Network of Family Systems Engineering practitioners who I have the privilege of working with for over five years.

Amidst growing concerns about the increasing number of couples that experience crises in the first few years of their marriage, this couple have been in the forefront of exploring new ways of preparing singles for marriage even before the choose the partner they will spend the rest of their lives with in marriage.

Their book, *RICA MODEL: The Pathway to A Fulfilling Marriage,* is a tool which young men and women can use to discover who they are, how they came to be and what type of partner will be a right fit for them.

The system and processes defined in the book have been practically tested in the field for over fifteen years. They have explained them in easy-to-understand language and the reader can follow the steps laid out in the book on their own.

Sola and Nike Ajayi, recognizing that application of knowledge is what brings about impact to the reader of any book of this nature, included a chapter titled Application to encourage the reader to actually apply what they learn from reading the book.

I particularly commend them for including worksheets and exercises in the appendix which support the reader's efforts toward applying the concepts shared in the book.

I encourage the singles and newly married couples to read and use this book. It will equip them to lay a solid foundation for healthy and long lasting marriages.

I also encourage parents and grandparents to read this book. It will help them have meaningful conversations which their children and grandchildren well ahead of a decision to marry. It will also equip them to provide the right kind of support and encouragement for their adult children and wards and they approach this life-impacting decision.

RICA MODEL: The Pathway to A Fulfilling Marriage is a book that will definitely reduce the apprehension that many men and women have about marriage.

Modupe Ehirim
Founder & Lead Counsellor
The Right Fit Marriage Academy

Author's Note

The major reason we wrote this book is to replicate the ideas, values, virtues, experiences, and passion for marriage, more endearingly, into the lives of young adults. One major thing that lives on is books. Books are legacies that live on even after the author's demise, and just as the Bible quotes in Proverbs 10:7, *"Good people leave memories that bless us." ERV.*

God gave us a promise and a gift but we have to intentionally invest in it to expand our knowledge and save more marriages. This is us pouring our lives; our experiences that begat understanding; our love and passion for marriage into this life-changing piece you are holding in your hand.

This book is set to transform marriages in the upcoming generations. So, if you are in a If you are in a serious, committed relationship and are about to get married or your marriage is less than five years old, this is the right book for you. Relax, read, and practice so you don't stumble and struggle into marriage, and if married, watch how enjoyable your marriage becomes.

Content

INTRODUCTION

"Marriage: a bond between two people who fall in love and decide to spend the rest of their lives together." It sounds simple, doesn't it? The idea of finding your soulmate, walking down the aisle, and living "happily ever after" is a dream many of us hold dear. But as anyone who has been in a committed relationship knows, it is not always that easy.

In this book, we are going to explore the intricacies of marriage and the challenges that couples face in our modern society, and we will introduce you to a structured approach that can transform your marriage into a fulfilling and lasting partnership. Welcome to "The RICA Model: The Pathway to a Fulfilling Marriage."

The Importance of a Blissful Marriage

Marriage is one of the most profound and life-altering decisions you can make. It is a commitment to share your life, dreams, and everything in between with another person. When it works, it is a source of incredible joy, support, and personal growth. But when it falters, it can lead to heartbreak, disappointment, and profound emotional pain.

The importance of a blissful marriage cannot be overstated. Why? Because the quality of your marriage often spills over into every aspect of your life. When your relationship is harmonious, your mental and emotional well-being thrives. You are more productive at work, a better parent to your children, and a more supportive friend. Conversely, when your marriage is troubled, it can become a source of stress that seeps into all other areas of your life.

Think of marriage as the foundation of a happy and fulfilling life. It is the sturdy base upon which you build your hopes, dreams, and aspirations. Just as a solid foundation is essential for a sturdy house, a strong marriage is essential for a fulfilling life.

Yet, the truth is that maintaining a blissful marriage is not always easy. In the whirlwind of modern life, we often forget to nurture our relationships. We get caught up in careers, daily routines, and the endless distractions of the digital age. We neglect the very bond that once brought us together in love.

In this fast-paced world, it is crucial to take a step back and understand that a blissful marriage does not just happen. It is something you must actively work on and invest in, just like any other aspect of your life if you want to succeed. So, why do so many marriages today struggle, and what are the challenges couples face in our modern society?

The Challenges Couples Face in Modern Society

Our anchor Scripture for this book is Proverbs 24:3–4 (KJV) and it reads: *"Through wisdom is a house builded; And by understanding it is established: And by knowledge shall the chambers be filled With all precious and pleasant riches."*

From this verses, the RICA Model came to life. Here is a breakdown of it.

Wisdom means Application.
Understanding means Comprehension.
Knowledge means Information.
The **house** means Revelation.

When a marriage is built without the RICA Model as seen in our anchor Scripture, challenges arise.

The challenges facing couples in today's world are complex and multifaceted. While every marriage is unique and has its own set of issues, some common trends and challenges seem to be affecting couples universally.

- *Communication Breakdown:* In the age of smartphones, social media, and constant connectivity, it's paradoxical that many couples struggle to communicate effectively. We are more connected than ever, yet we often fail to truly connect with our partners. Misunderstandings, arguments, and emotional distance can erode the very foundation of a marriage.

- *Work-Life Balance:* The demands of modern careers can be all-consuming. Balancing work and family life is a constant struggle for many couples. Long hours at the office, business trips, and the pressure to succeed can take a toll on your relationship.

- *Financial Stress:* Money is a common source of tension in marriages. Disagreements about budgeting, spending habits, and financial goals can lead to arguments and resentment.

- *Changing Gender Roles:* As societal norms evolve, so do the roles and expectations within marriages. Traditional gender roles are shifting, and couples are navigating new dynamics that can be challenging to adjust to.

- *Parenting Pressures:* Raising children is a beautiful and rewarding experience, but it can also be incredibly demanding. The stress of parenting, coupled with differing parenting styles, can strain a marriage.

- *Technology and Social Media:* The digital age has introduced a new set of challenges. Social media can lead to jealousy and insecurity, while excessive screen time can create physical and emotional distance.

- Lack of Quality Time: In the hustle and bustle of modern life, couples often find themselves with less quality time for each other. This lack of connection can lead to feelings of neglect and isolation.

- *Unrealistic Expectations:* Romantic comedies, fairy tales, and social media often portray idealised versions of love and marriage. These unrealistic expectations can leave couples feeling dissatisfied with their relationships.

It is necessary to acknowledge that these challenges are not insurmountable. Every marriage faces hurdles, but it is how you address and overcome them that determines the health and longevity of your relationship.

So, how can couples navigate the complex landscape of modern marriage successfully? The answer lies in adopting a structured approach – a roadmap, if you will – based on the RICA (Revelation, Information, Comprehension, and Application) Model for building and maintaining a strong and blissful marriage.

The RICA Model is not just a theoretical framework; it is a practical guide based on real-world experiences and research. It is designed to provide couples with a clear and actionable path to building and maintaining a strong and fulfilling marriage.

In the chapters that follow, we will delve deep into each of these pillars, offering practical advice, real-life stories, and exercises to help you strengthen your marriage. The RICA Model is not a one-size-fits-all solution but rather a customizable framework that you can tailor to your unique relationship.

We will explore the art of Revelation through fellowship with The Source, the acquisition of Information for better understanding, Comprehension of your partner's needs, and the Application of strategies to adapt to changing circumstances. Whether you are in the early stages of your relationship or celebrating a milestone anniversary, The RICA Model can guide you toward the thriving marriage you have always desired.

PART ONE

REVELATION

1

Revelation: The Guiding Light

Revelation is communication from God to His children on the earth and one of the great blessings associated with the gift and constant companionship of the Holy Ghost.

Life can be like a complex puzzle, and sometimes, we need that special light to show us the way. In the pursuit of a happy marriage, that guiding light is called "Revelation."

In a world full of opinions and distractions, figuring out love and marriage can feel like navigating a confusing maze. Many of us dive into relationships without a clear sense of direction, and that is where revelation comes in. It is like having a divine GPS that helps you make sense of it all.

Revelation is about connecting with God, the ultimate source of love and wisdom. It is about seeking His guidance and listening to His whispers amid the noise of the world. When you embrace revelation, you are letting

God take the wheel on your journey to a meaningful and fulfilling marriage.

The Starting Point: Your Relationship with God

It all begins with your relationship with God. Think of revelation as a conversation with a trusted friend. You have to know their voice to understand what they are saying. Similarly, you need to know God's voice to grasp His guidance.

"My sheep listen to my voice; I know them, and they follow me." - *John 10:27 (NIV)*

This verse reminds us of the special bond between God and His people. Just as sheep recognize their shepherd's voice, we too can recognize God's voice. But like any good relationship, it takes time and effort to get to that point.

As we move forward, you will see that revelation is not some mysterious thing reserved for a select few. It is like a gift waiting for anyone who wants it. It is the tool that can help you navigate the world of relationships and lead you to a marriage filled with love and purpose.

Are you prepared to invite God into your quest for a fulfilling marriage?

2

Our Journey Of Revelation

The journey of a thousand miles

starts with the first step...

21st November 1999 was when the journey started and just as the Bible recorded that the Earth was without form, this was a formless journey as I remember it.

This gentleman had been asking me out, trying to win my heart, trying to make me love him as much as he does me or at least make me see how much he does. One of the days came and after much consideration, questions in my heart, prayers and counselling, at 8 p.m. that saying the University of Ado-Ekiti, I said "Yes" to him. I agreed to court him and guess what happened next.

He took my hand, led me to one of the fields in my school to pray and commit our courtship into the hands of God. There was a conviction that this wasn't just an ordinary courtship and somehow, we knew that our relationship was going to end up in marriage.

While we were praying, the WORD came to us that our home would be a role model home to other homes. On that note, we started the courtship, unintentionally but with the word of God which is the most intentional thing (tool) one can ever have in life. We did not know the step by step to making our home a role model. Just like Abraham who had no child, God called him a father of many nations. God spoke about our home being a model for other homes while I was still single... I had not even gotten married.

The vision became clear when we remembered how much both of us (my husband and I) desired a home better than the home we came from. My husband especially is from a polygamous home and he had asked God, even before he met me, that he never wanted a marriage like his father's. Based on that, we came together and we started off our kind of courtship and God has been faithful.

So many years went by, years of courtship and heart of marriage. It took 5 years of courtship and 5 years of marriage before we remembered that there were no misunderstandings and quarrels. Five years into our marriage, we never had any quarrels, misunderstandings or conflicts of any sort. At the time while we were still courting, a close friend of ours asked about how we manage issues between ourselves and then, just then did we remember that there were things that could cause conflicts between couples. It never crossed our minds, we never thought of how it would happen or even what if it happened. It was as though something was missing in our relationship and that question activated an expectation for a quarrel.

There's this popular saying that goes..."When two friends stay together for a while and never quarrel, it means they never told themselves the truth." It makes sense when it means there is bound to be even the slightest argument over a misunderstanding or just a simple disagreement but to the glory of God, we have never had a single quarrel.

After we got married, we never fancied the idea of getting religious artefacts such as frames with the image of Jesus or a wooden cross, we were just satisfied that we had God on our side and even after marriage, we still got testimonies of how calm and peaceful our home feels from visiting friends.

On a particular occasion when a friend expressed how peaceful it feels whenever she steps into our home, she explained how much of the presence of God she feels each time she visits. At that point was when we remembered what God said and we realised that it could be a common thing to act in the face of visitors as if there were no issues and it is another thing to not have a single issue. The latter was our story.

There was truly never a misunderstanding. It was so unusual because it wasn't our doing. Humanly speaking, we would have had our share of ups and downs in marriage but it was God's doing; it is a script originally written by God and it was not written for us but for other marriages.

3

Go To The Source

You know, it is not God's desire to conceal but to reveal. The word revelation means "unveiling."

— Greg Laurie

Imagine embarking on a road trip without a GPS or a map. You would be driving aimlessly, hoping to stumble upon your destination. This scenario closely mirrors how some individuals approach the pursuit of marriage. They dive headfirst into the journey without a clear sense of direction or purpose.

In the context of the RICA Model, "Revelation" is like your divine GPS, guiding you on this life-altering journey. It is about connecting with God, seeking His guidance, and allowing Him to lead the way. Whether you are currently single or in a relationship, having a personal relationship with God is paramount.

A Relationship with God: More Than a Checklist

Now, you might be thinking, "I attend church regularly and pray occasionally; isn't that enough?" Well, while attending church and praying are certainly important, a true relationship with God goes beyond these routine activities. It is about knowing Him intimately and recognizing His voice when He speaks.

"My sheep listen to my voice; I know them, and they follow me." - John 10:27 (NIV)*

Imagine you are in a crowded room, and someone you know whispers your name. You can pick out their voice amid the chatter. Similarly, as God's child, you should be like sheep who recognize their Shepherd's voice. It is not a skill you develop overnight. It requires a consistent, ongoing relationship with Him.

Koinonia: The Heart of Connection

In Greek, the word "koinonia" describes a deep, intimate fellowship. It is not merely a surface-level acquaintance; it is a profound connection. When it comes to your relationship with God, koinonia is the key.

"That which we have seen and heard we proclaim also to you, so that you too may have fellowship with us; and indeed

our fellowship is with the Father and with his Son Jesus Christ." - 1 John 1:3 (ESV)

Think of it this way: knowing someone's name and knowing their character, dreams, and desires are two different things. Koinonia with God involves seeking to understand Him at a profound level. It's about delving into the depths of His character, discovering His dreams for you, and aligning your desires with His.

The Revelation of God: Your Marital Blueprint

You might wonder, "Why is this level of intimacy with God so crucial to marriage?" The answer is simple: God is the ultimate source of wisdom, guidance, and love. When it comes to the sacred institution of marriage, He is the blueprint.

"For I know the plans I have for you, declares the LORD, plans for welfare and not for evil, to give you a future and a hope." - Jeremiah 29:11 (ESV)

In our society, we often seek advice from friends, self-help books, or even therapists when it comes to relationships. While these resources can be valuable, there is nothing quite like consulting the Creator of Love Himself. God knows you better than anyone else, and He knows your potential partner equally well.

By seeking revelation from God, you gain access to His divine wisdom. He can reveal whether a person is right for you or if it is time to move on. He can provide insights into compatibility, character, and shared purpose. His guidance is like a lighthouse, showing you the way through the stormy seas of dating and relationships.

Timing Is Everything

One mistake many people make is waiting until they are on the brink of marriage to start seeking God's guidance. It's like preparing for a marathon the night before the race. You wouldn't do that, would you?

Similarly, your relationship with God should be cultivated long before you start thinking about marriage. Think of it as training for the race of a lifetime. The more time you spend getting to know God, the better equipped you will be to hear His voice when it truly matters.

How to Cultivate Revelation

How can you cultivate revelation in your life? Here are some practical steps:

1. *Start with Prayer:* Prayer is your direct line to God. It is where you can pour out your heart, express your desires, and seek His guidance.

2. *Study the Word:* The Bible is God's love letter to humanity. It is a source of wisdom, comfort, and revelation. Dive into its pages and let God speak to you through His Word.

3. *Listen in Silence*: In our noisy world, it is essential to find moments of silence. Sometimes, God speaks in whispers. Take time to listen to His gentle voice.

4. *Seek Godly Counsel:* Surround yourself with wise, God-fearing individuals who can provide guidance and support in your journey.

5. *Practice Obedience:* When God speaks, act on His guidance. Obedience is the key to deeper revelation.

6. Stay Patient: Revelation doesn't always come instantaneously. Be patient and trust in God's timing.

In the pursuit of a fulfilling marriage, revelation is your compass, your guiding light. It is about fostering a deep, intimate relationship with God, seeking His wisdom, and allowing Him to lead you in the realm of love and relationships. Remember, it is not just about knowing who God is; it is about knowing Him personally and recognizing His voice when He calls.

Marriage, this beautiful union between two souls, is too important to embark upon without divine guidance. So, start today. Cultivate your relationship with God, seek His revelation, and let Him be your ultimate source of wisdom and love on this incredible journey toward a fulfilling marriage.

PART TWO

INFORMATION

Information: The Lifeblood

"Adventure can be an end in itself. Self-discovery is the secret ingredient that fuels daring."

—Grace Lichtenstein

Picture this: Information is the lifeblood of your marriage, coursing through its veins and breathing life into every moment you spend together. It is not just about knowing the basics, like your partner's favourite ice cream flavour or their peculiar habit of leaving their socks everywhere. No, it goes much deeper than that. Information in a marriage encompasses the entirety of your partner's being, from their innermost desires to their hidden fears, from the dreams they nurture to the wounds they carry. It is this vast and intricate web of knowledge that forms the foundation of your connection.

So, why does this matter? How you communicate and absorb information within your marriage can be the linchpin that determines its success or failure. Think of it as a dynamic dance of understanding, trust, and empathy. Imagine your marriage as a beautiful tapestry, woven from the threads of shared experiences, emotions, and aspirations. Each piece of information you exchange is a thread that adds depth and richness to this tapestry, making it a masterpiece that is uniquely yours.

As you embark on this journey of sharing and learning within your marriage, remember that it is not about being perfect but about being present. It is about making the effort to truly know and understand your partner, even as both of you continue to grow and change. It is about weaving a tapestry of love, trust, and shared experiences that will stand the test of time.

In the upcoming chapters of "The RICA Model: The Pathway to a Fulfilling Marriage," we will delve even deeper into the fascinating world of information in marriage. We will explore practical exercises and insightful anecdotes that will help you master the art of sharing and learning, ultimately enriching your connection with your beloved partner.

Self-Discovery

"You have no need to travel anywhere. Journey within yourself, enter a mine of rubies and bathe in the splendour of your own light."

—Rumi

Think of self-discovery as the ignition key that starts the engine of transformation in your quest for a fulfilling marriage. It is the process of getting to know yourself deeply, not just on the surface but in the hidden corners of your heart and mind. Self-discovery is like exploring a treasure chest within yourself, uncovering your strengths, weaknesses, dreams, and fears. It is a journey that can be both exciting and challenging, but it is worth every step.

Self-Awareness: The Mirror of Your Soul

Self-awareness is the first milestone on the road to self-discovery. It is like holding up a mirror to your soul and taking a long, hard look. To embark on this journey effectively, you need to answer some fundamental questions:

1. Who Are You?: Beyond your name, job title, and social status, who are you at your core? What values, beliefs and principles define you? What are your passions and interests that make you unique?

2. What Are Your Strengths and Weaknesses?: We all have them, and acknowledging them is the first step towards personal growth. What are you great at? What areas of your life could use improvement?

3. What Are Your Dreams and Aspirations?: Have you ever taken the time to define your dreams and set goals for yourself? What do you want to achieve in life, both personally and professionally?

4. What Are Your Fears and Insecurities?: These are the stumbling blocks that can hinder your journey towards a fulfilling marriage. Identifying your fears is the first step in conquering them.

5. What Makes You Happy and What Drains Your Energy?: Knowing what brings you joy and what saps your vitality is essential for creating a life that aligns with your true self.

Self-awareness is not about judgement or criticism; it is about understanding and acceptance. It's about seeing yourself as you truly are and making peace with your imperfections while celebrating your strengths.

Self Realisation: Embracing Your Authentic Self

Once you have embarked on the path of self-awareness, the next step is self-realisation. This is where you take all that self-knowledge and apply it to your life. It is about living authentically and aligning your actions with your values and aspirations.

Here are some essential aspects of self-realisation:

1. Authenticity: Be true to yourself. Do not pretend to be someone you are not to fit into a mould or meet someone else's expectations. Authenticity is magnetic; it attracts people who appreciate you for who you are.

2. Personal Growth: Embrace opportunities for personal growth and development. This might involve pursuing further education, learning new skills, or simply working on your emotional intelligence.

3. Healthy Relationships: Surround yourself with people who uplift and support you. Toxic relationships can hinder your journey towards self-realisation, so it is

crucial to recognize and distance yourself from them.

4. Self-Care: Prioritise self-care in your life. Taking care of your physical, emotional, and mental well-being is vital for becoming the best version of yourself.

5. Setting Boundaries: Learn to set healthy boundaries in your relationships. Boundaries protect your emotional and mental space, ensuring you do not compromise your values or well-being for others.

Understanding Your Singlehood

Understanding your singlehood is essential because it lays the groundwork for a successful transition into marriage.

Singlehood is not a waiting room for marriage; it is a unique phase of life that deserves your attention and appreciation. Here is how to navigate it:

1. Enjoy Independence: Singlehood is an excellent time to revel in your independence. Explore your interests, travel, take risks, and make memories that are uniquely yours.

2. Learn From Past Relationships: Reflect on your past relationships, both the successful and unsuccessful ones. What did you learn about yourself and what you are looking for in a partner? Use this knowledge to refine

your relationship criteria.

3. Build a Support Network: Surround yourself with friends and loved ones who understand and respect your singlehood. A strong support network provides emotional stability and companionship.

4. Work on Your Self-Esteem: Your self-esteem is the foundation of healthy relationships. Use this time to boost your self-confidence and self-worth through self-love and self-care practices.

5. Set Relationship Goals: Define what you want in a future partner and relationship. Be specific about your values, expectations, and deal-breakers. This clarity will guide you when you start dating.

Singlehood versus Marriage-ability

It is crucial to address a common misconception: Singlehood does not equate to being unmarriageable. In fact, singlehood can be a valuable time for personal growth and preparation for a successful marriage. Let's break down some myths and truths:

Myth 1: Being Single Equals Unmarriageable.
False. Singlehood is not a reflection of your worthiness for marriage. It is simply a phase in life. Many people

enter marriage after spending significant time as single individuals. It is about finding the right partner at the right time, not rushing into a relationship because society says you should.

Myth 2: You Must Be Perfect to Get Married.

False. Perfection is an illusion. Everyone has flaws and imperfections. A healthy and fulfilling marriage is built on acceptance and love for each other's imperfections. Being true to yourself and working on personal growth are more important than striving for perfection.

Myth 3: Marriage Fixes Everything.

False. Marriage is not a magic wand that solves all your problems. In fact, it amplifies existing issues. It is essential to address your personal challenges and baggage before entering a marriage to ensure a solid foundation.

Truth 1: Self-Discovery Enhances Marriage-ability.

True. Understanding yourself, your values, and your needs is a powerful tool for finding a compatible partner and nurturing a fulfilling marriage. It enables you to communicate effectively, resolve conflicts, and make decisions that align with your shared vision.

Truth 2: Healthy Singlehood Leads to a Healthy Marriage.

True. A well-lived singlehood can contribute positively to your marriage. It allows you to develop self-reliance, independence, and emotional resilience—all valuable qualities in a partnership.

Self-discovery is the key to unlocking your potential for a fulfilling marriage. Self-awareness and self-realisation help you become the best version of yourself while understanding your singlehood sets the stage for a successful transition into marriage. Remember, singlehood is not a waiting game; it is a unique and valuable phase of life. Embrace it fully, and you will be well-prepared for the beautiful journey of marriage ahead.

6

Intrapersonal Relationship Over Interpersonal Relationship

Work on your relationships...

Relationships need renewal or they die.

The traditional view of marriage often emphasizes the importance of interpersonal dynamics—the interactions between spouses, communication skills, and conflict resolution strategies. While these aspects are undoubtedly crucial, they can only flourish when you first nurture our intrapersonal relationship—the relationship you have with yourself.

So, why the emphasis on intrapersonal over interpersonal? Because it is within you that we carry your beliefs, values, and emotional baggage. If you are not in tune with your inner self, how can you possibly create a thriving partnership with someone else?

Building a healthy intrapersonal relationship involves four steps - Reflection, introspection, communication, and action (R.I.C.A.).

Reflection - Know Thyself

In the age-old quest for a fulfilling marriage, self-awareness is the first step. We often enter relationships without fully understanding our own needs, desires, and emotional triggers. The result? We bring unresolved baggage into our marriages, hoping that our partner will help us unpack it. But it does not work that way.

Take the time to look within and understand who you are as an individual. What are your values, dreams, and aspirations? What makes you tick, and what makes you uneasy? By gaining clarity on these aspects, you will be better equipped to communicate your needs and expectations to your partner, setting the stage for a healthier marriage.

Introspection - Healing the Self

Once you have reflected on your own identity and the experiences that have shaped you, it is time to move on to introspection. We all carry emotional wounds from the past, and these can have a significant impact on our marriages.

Through introspection, you will learn how to identify and address these wounds. Whether it is past traumas, insecurities, or unresolved conflicts, remember that a strong intrapersonal relationship is built on a foundation of self-love and acceptance. By addressing your own emotional baggage, you will be better prepared to support your partner in doing the same.

Communication - The Bridge to Connection

Now that you have laid the groundwork with reflection and introspection, it is time to turn your attention to the interpersonal relationship aspect. Communication is often touted as the key to a successful marriage, and for good reason. But not all communication is created equal.

Communication is not just about talking; it is about truly listening, understanding, and empathizing with yourself. Have open and honest conversations with yourself and others, listen actively, and be vulnerable.

When you understand yourself better, you can express your needs and emotions more clearly, which in turn fosters a deeper connection with your spouse.

Action - Growing Together

For every success, change is inevitable. People grow, circumstances evolve, and you must adapt accordingly.

Take action. For every lesson learnt, implement and execute. Do not be a decider alone, be a doer. When you make a decision, take actions that back it up and bring it to fruition.

By prioritizing your intrapersonal relationship and fostering a deep connection with yourself, you can build a strong foundation for a loving and lasting partnership with your spouse.

Intrapersonal relationships are the cornerstone of any successful interpersonal relationship. By understanding and nurturing your own needs, emotions, and growth, you can create a solid foundation for a thriving marriage. The RICA Model is not a quick fix but a lifelong journey toward fulfillment, connection, and love. It's time to embark on this path and discover the endless possibilities that await you and your partner.

Emotional Wholeness

"One of the best things you can do for yourself is to protect your emotional health."

- Angel Moreira

Marriage is a script originally written by God but still needs two earthly individuals to make it happen—to act out the script. These individuals have a couple of differences in areas like how they grew up, the kind of family they came from, their experiences, how they were brought up, effects of their surroundings, and how their lives were shaped intentionally and otherwise. There is a difference in choices, tastes, opinions, ideologies, ways of life, resolutions, and beliefs that has shaped the lives of these individuals.

An individual is a person considered alone rather than belonging to a group of people. It could also be defined as a single physical human being. The keywords to consider are "ALONE" and "SINGLE". There can only be "two" if there are "ones" to be put together; there cannot be a double without a single; and likewise, there cannot be a together without first being alone.

Before considering marriage or while considering it, take time out to develop yourself in a solo manner. Don't focus on the kind of spouse you want; focus on the kind of spouse you would like to be and work towards it.

Getting Whole And Ready

Getting whole talks about a couple of other things, but let us focus on getting whole for marriage. How does one get whole and ready for marriage, you may ask?

As earlier stated, focus on the kind of spouse you would like to be—that is, the kind of wife you want to be to your husband, or the kind of husband you want to be to your wife. Decide to be a better person than you were yesterday, last week, or last year. Make a list of your strengths and weaknesses, or shortcomings, and take significant time out to work on them. Don't work on them in passing. Weaknesses are not meant to be ignored; work on them; likewise, strengths are not meant to be overestimated; keep them under constant check. Take personality report tests to see for yourself the kind of spouse you would make. Ask random and specific questions about yourself from friends (trusted friends) and family members.

Doing all these could help in two areas. The first is in the area of attracting who you are. A popular saying goes "We attract who we are on the inside" and the Bible also states that "the deep calls upon the deep". When you work on yourself to get better and you actually do get better, you attract someone who is close to who you are or someone who complements who you are.

In the second area, making yourself whole will result in a whole home. When you work on yourself, find yourself, overcome your weaknesses, master your strengths, and become a better you before getting married, you would have ruled out the chance of stumbling into marriage. After you've taken all these tests and answered all the questions, you ask the ultimate question about marriage.

"IF I MET SOMEONE EXACTLY AS I AM AS AN OPPOSITE SEX, WOULD I GO AHEAD WITH THE MARRIAGE PLANS?"

If your answer is no, you would have to review yourself again. Ask questions about those things that you cannot tolerate in someone else and can find in yourself. Make findings on why you wouldn't want to marry yourself and work on them. Do these tests and findings over and over again, as much as you can, until you can answer "yes" to that question.

Nurturing Emotional Intelligence and Empathy

Empathy is the greatest virtue. From it, all virtues flow. Without it, all virtues are an act.

– Eric Zorn

While it might sound like something reserved for psychologists and self-help gurus, "emotional intelligence" is an essential component of any healthy marriage. Think of it as your ability to recognize, understand, and manage your emotions and those of your partner.

Imagine this: You have had a rough day at work, and you come home feeling frustrated and exhausted. Your spouse, with high emotional intelligence, picks up on your mood without you uttering a single word. They offer a listening ear and a comforting presence, allowing you to vent and release your pent-up emotions.

Now, contrast this with a scenario where your spouse fails to notice your emotional turmoil or, worse yet, responds negatively, escalating the tension. This is where emotional intelligence comes into play, helping you navigate the emotional landscape of your marriage.

The Power of Empathy

Closely linked to emotional intelligence is empathy, often described as the ability to understand and share the feelings of another. Empathy is the secret sauce that binds couples together through thick and thin. It is about more than just recognizing emotions; it is about truly connecting with your partner on an emotional level.

Empathy is not a switch you can flip on and off at will. It requires practice and genuine care for your partner's well-being. When you are empathetic, you step into your partner's shoes, seeing the world through their eyes, feeling their joys and sorrows as if they were your own.

When your spouse has a bad day, empathy allows you to be there for them, providing the comfort and support they need. It is saying, "I understand what you're going through, and I'm here for you." This powerful affirmation can make all the difference in your marriage.

Insights into Your Partner's Needs and Desires

In the fast-paced whirlwind of daily life, it is easy to lose sight of what truly matters in your marriage. Sometimes, we forget that our partners have their own sets of needs, desires, and dreams. To build a fulfilling marriage, it is essential to gain insights into what makes your partner tick.

Start by asking questions, engaging in deep conversations, and actively listening to your partner. What are their goals and aspirations? What are their fears and insecurities? What makes them happy and what makes them sad? Understanding these facets of your partner's inner world can strengthen the bonds of your relationship.

One important aspect of understanding your partner's needs is realising that they may change over time. Life circumstances, personal growth, and evolving priorities can all impact what your partner desires from the relationship. Thus, it is vital to maintain open and ongoing communication to stay attuned to these changes.

Responsiveness Versus Reactivity

In the bustling city of Lagos lived two couples, the Parkers and the Adams. They each faced a situation that highlighted the difference between being responsive and reactive.

The Parkers: John came home after a tough day at work, visibly upset. He had received some negative feedback from his boss, and it weighed heavily on his mind. Seeing John's distress, Maria immediately set aside her plans. She asked gently, "What's bothering you, dear?"

John shared his concerns, and Maria listened attentively without judgement. She empathised with his frustration. After he had vented, she said, "I understand how that must have been difficult for you. Let's discuss how we can address this together."

The Parkers' responsiveness built trust and emotional closeness. They worked as a team to resolve John's work-related stress, strengthening their bond.

On the other side of the neighbourhood lived the Adams, Sarah and Michael. One morning, Sarah discovered that Michael had forgotten their anniversary, and she exploded in anger. "You never listen to me! You don't care about our relationship!" she shouted.

Michael felt attacked and reacted defensively, saying, "You're always overreacting. It's just one day."
Their argument escalated, and the day that should have celebrated their love ended in tears and resentment.

The Adams' reactivity strained their relationship. Hurtful words were exchanged, making it harder to find common ground.

Over time, both couples learned vital lessons. The Parkers continued to prioritise responsiveness, nurturing their connection. They faced challenges together with understanding and support.

The Adams recognized the destructive power of reactivity. They sought help and learned to pause before reacting, listening with empathy. Gradually, they began rebuilding trust and communication.

In the heat of the moment, we often react without thinking. We say things we do not mean, lash out in frustration, or shut down emotionally. These knee-jerk reactions can have detrimental effects on your marriage. That is where responsiveness comes in as a healthier alternative.

Responsiveness involves pausing before reacting and considering the impact of your words and actions. It is about choosing empathy and emotional intelligence over impulsivity. When your partner shares their thoughts or feelings, take a moment to reflect and respond thoughtfully.

At the end of the story of the Parkers and the Adams, we see the importance of responsiveness in relationships. It fosters trust and closeness, while reactivity often leads to misunderstanding and conflict. The Parkers and the Adams carried these lessons with them, working to create healthier and more fulfilling connections in their lives.

Strategies for Effective Information Sharing and Learning in Marriage

Marriage is a lifelong journey of growth and discovery, and effective information sharing and learning are key components of that journey. Let's explore some practical strategies to enhance these aspects of your relationship.

1. Cultivate Active Listening

Active listening is the foundation of effective communication. When your partner speaks, give them your full attention. Put away distractions, maintain eye contact, and show that you are fully present. Encourage your partner to express their thoughts and feelings without interruption. Once they have finished, paraphrase what you have heard to ensure understanding.

2. Embrace Vulnerability

Vulnerability is not a sign of weakness; it is a sign of strength and trust. Share your thoughts, fears, and dreams openly with your partner. When you open up, you invite your spouse to do the same, deepening your connection and understanding.

3. Practise Regular Check-Ins

Set aside time for regular check-ins with your partner. These can be weekly or monthly sessions where you discuss your relationship, your individual needs, and your shared goals. It is an opportunity to ensure you're both on the same page and to address any concerns that may have arisen.

4. Seek Feedback and Adapt

Ask for feedback from your partner on how you can improve as a spouse. Be open to constructive criticism and willing to adapt your behaviour. Remember, marriage is a journey of growth, and both partners must be willing to evolve and change.

5. Use "I" Statements

When discussing issues or concerns, frame your thoughts using "I" statements instead of accusatory language. For example, say "I feel hurt when..." instead of "You always make me feel...". This approach minimises defensiveness and encourages a more productive conversation.

6. Celebrate Each Other's Achievements

Share in each other's successes, no matter how small. Celebrate your partner's accomplishments and milestones, and offer support during challenging times. This reinforces a sense of togetherness and partnership in your marriage.

7. Prioritise Quality Time

In our busy lives, it is easy to let quality time with your spouse slip through the cracks. Make a conscious effort to spend time together without distractions. Whether it is a cosy dinner at home, a weekend getaway, or a simple walk in the park, these moments strengthen your bond.

Emotional intelligence, empathy, understanding your partner's needs and desires, and effective communication are the building blocks of a fulfilling marriage. They lay the foundation for trust, love, and lasting happiness. Remember, marriage is not a destination but a journey, and it's a journey worth investing in. So, nurture these qualities, practise these strategies, and watch your marriage thrive.

PART THREE

COMPREHENSION

Comprehension: The Cornerstone

The best part of love when you understand her without telling anything.

Comprehension, in its essence, is the key to understanding. But here is the thing—it is not just about understanding your partner or your relationship. It is about comprehending yourself, your partner, and the world around you. Think of it as a universal decoder ring that enables you to decipher the intricate messages life sends your way.

Picture this for a moment: you're sitting across from your partner, sipping your morning coffee, and you suddenly find yourself asking, "Why do they always leave their socks on the floor?" Or perhaps, "What's going on inside their head when they have a tough day at work?" These questions are the seeds of comprehension, and they have the power to transform your relationship.

Comprehension, at its core, is about curiosity, empathy, and the willingness to peel back the layers of your partner's world and your own. It is about becoming a detective of emotions, a connoisseur of thoughts, and a master of communication. But don't worry; you don't need a magnifying glass or a degree in psychology to get started. All you need is an open heart and a commitment to deepening your connection.

Imagine comprehension as a beautiful tapestry woven from threads of self-awareness and understanding. When you take the time to comprehend yourself, you gain valuable insights into your needs, desires, and fears. This self-awareness serves as a solid foundation for a healthy and fulfilling marriage because, as they say, you can't truly love another until you love yourself.

But comprehension does not stop at self-discovery. It extends to your partner as well. When you make an effort to understand their thoughts, feelings, and experiences, you are essentially extending a hand of empathy and creating a safe space for them to do the same. This reciprocity forms the backbone of a strong and lasting connection.

We are all unique individuals, shaped by our past experiences, values, and dreams. Our perceptions, motivations, and even our quirks can be vastly different. Comprehension bridges these gaps, allowing you to navigate the complexities of your partner's world with grace and compassion.

You might be wondering, "How do I put comprehension into action in my marriage?" The answer is delightfully simple: through communication. In "The RICA Model," we explore practical tools and techniques that empower you to engage in meaningful conversations with your partner.

Think of comprehension as the key that unlocks the treasure chest of your partner's inner world. When you ask questions like, "How was your day?" or "What are your dreams for the future?" you're inviting them to share their hopes, fears, and aspirations. You are showing them that their thoughts and feelings matter, that their voice is heard and that their presence is cherished.

But comprehension is not just about understanding the present; it is also a tool for navigating the future. As life evolves, so do we and our relationships. "The RICA Model" equips you with the skills to adapt and grow together, nurturing a marriage that remains fulfilling through the years.

Comprehension is not a destination; it is a lifelong

endeavour. It is a commitment to continually learn, evolve, and deepen your connection with your partner. It is about celebrating the uniqueness of your love story and finding joy in the ever-unfolding chapters.

10

Understanding Times & Seasons

None of us knows what will happen next moment, yet we move forward. Because we trust.

Because there is faith in us.

In the journey of life, one thing becomes apparent: timing is everything. It is the thread that weaves through the fabric of our existence, guiding us through the seasons of growth, change, and fulfillment. Just as nature's rhythms teach us the art of patience, so do our relationships require us to grasp the essence of timing.

The Bible offers timeless wisdom on this very subject, stating in Ecclesiastes 3:1 (NIV), *"There is a time for everything, and a season for every activity under the heavens."* These words hold profound significance in our quest for a fulfilling marriage. Understanding the times and seasons of your relationship is paramount, much like recognizing when the mangoes in your orchard are ripe for picking.

Our journey to understanding times and seasons begins with Ecclesiastes, a book in the Bible often attributed to King Solomon. His words echo through the ages, reminding us that there is a time and season for every aspect of our lives, including marriage. As nature follows a distinct pattern, so do relationships.

The First Chapter of Ecclesiastes opens with these profound words:

"To everything, there is a season, a time for every purpose under heaven: a time to be born, and a time to die; a time to plant, and a time to pluck what is planted; a time to kill, and a time to heal; a time to break down, and a time to build up; a time to weep, and a time to laugh; a time to mourn, and a time to dance..."(Ecclesiastes 3:1-4, NKJV)

These verses encapsulate the essence of the RICA Model — recognizing that every moment has its purpose, and every season has its unique beauty and challenges.

The Rica Model For Understanding Times And Seasons

R - Recognize:

The same way you recognise a ripe fruit, you must recognize the current season of your relationship or marriage. Is it a season of growth, change, or stability?

"Recognizing" the season of your relationship or marriage is like surveying your mango orchard and assessing the stage of each tree. Fruits do not ripen overnight, your relationship will also not move from one season to the next in the blink of an eye. Let's break down the concept of recognizing the season:

Early Season: This early season is a time of growth, where you plant the seeds of your shared life.

Mid-Season: This is where you cultivate the love and connection that will sustain you.

Late Season: In this seasaon, appreciate the depth of your connection and enjoy the fruits of your labor.

I - Invest:

Investing time in your marriage helps you stay strong through the different seasons of life that you have to go through. This may iinclude strengthening your communication, trust, or intimacy.

Here's how you can apply the "Invest" aspect of the RICA Model:

Time: Dedicate quality time to your spouse. In the early season, this might involve getting to know each other deeply. In the mid-season, it could mean maintaining routines that nurture your bond. In the late season, it's about cherishing every moment together.

Communication: Open and honest communication is the nutrient-rich soil in which your relationship grows. Share your thoughts, feelings, and dreams with your partner. Listening is equally important, as it helps you understand each other's needs and desires.

Trust: Trust is the sturdy branch that supports your relationship or marriage through all seasons. Build trust by keeping your promises, being reliable, and addressing issues with empathy and respect.

Intimacy: Intimacy is the sweet nectar that enhances your connection. It's not just about physical closeness but also emotional intimacy. Be vulnerable with each other and allow your love to deepen.

C - Cultivate:

Cultivating your relationship is similar to tending to plants, it requires care and attention to thrive, so does your marriage. Here's how you can practice "Cultivate" in the RICA Model:

Address Issues: Address issues promptly. Discuss openly. Ignoring problems can lead to a decline in the relationship.

Nurture Love: Nurture the love you share by making an effort to keep the romance alive. Surprise your partner with gestures of affection, plan special dates, and find new ways to express your love.

Healthy Environment: Cultivate a loving atmosphere in your home. Without an atmosphere of love, care and trust, the marriage will be tough. Support each other's personal growth, and maintain a positive outlook.

Adaptability: Just as trees adapt to changing weather conditions, be adaptable in your relationship. Life throws curveballs, and the ability to adapt and support each other during challenging times is crucial.

A - Appreciate:

Cherish and celebrate the moments of joy, love, and connection in your marriage. Gratitude is a key component of a fulfilling relationship. Fully savour the moments of joy and connection in your marriage or relationship by doing the following.

Gratitude: Express gratitude daily for your partner and the love you share. Recognize the efforts and sacrifices made by both of you to nurture the relationship.

Celebrate Milestones: Celebrate the milestones in your marriage. Whether it is your anniversary, a personal achievement, or a simple moment of joy, commemorate these occasions.

Quality Time: In your relationship and marriage, prioritize quality time together. Create cherished memories by going on adventures, taking trips, or simply enjoying quiet moments together.

Reflection: Take time to reflect on your journey as a couple. Look back at how far you have come and the growth you have experienced. Reflecting on your love story can deepen your appreciation for each other.

Now that we have explored each component of the RICA Model, it is time to put it into action. The beauty of this model is its adaptability to your unique relationship. Just as mangoes ripen at their own pace, so do marriages. Here are some practical steps to apply the RICA Model in your marriage:

Assessment: Begin by assessing the current season of your marriage. Are you in an early, mid, or late season? This awareness will guide your actions.

Set Goals: Based on your assessment, set realistic goals for your relationship. What do you want to achieve in this season? What improvements or changes would you like to make?

Communication: Communicate your goals and intentions with your partner. Open dialogue is crucial to ensure you're both on the same page.

Consistency: Consistency is key in implementing the RICA Model. Make a commitment to invest, cultivate, and appreciate your relationship regularly, not just when problems arise.

Seek Support: If you encounter challenges along the way, don't hesitate to seek support from a trusted friend, family member, or a marriage counselor. Sometimes, an external perspective can provide valuable insights.

Adapt and Evolve: Remember that relationships, like seasons, change. Be willing to adapt the RICA Model to your evolving needs and circumstances.

By understanding the times and seasons of your

relationship, and by applying the principles of the RICA Model — Recognize, Invest, Cultivate, and Appreciate — you can nurture a fulfilling and enduring partnership.

In the words of Ecclesiastes 3:1 (NIV), *"There is a time for everything, and a season for every activity under the heavens."* Embrace the seasons of your marriage, for within them lies the beauty, growth, and sweetness of your shared journey.

11

Building a Deeper Understanding With Your Partner

"We are all unique. Understand rather than judge."

While the idea of marriage may have once seemed like a simple declaration of love, the truth is that sustaining a thriving marriage is a complex art. It is not just about exchanging vows and hoping for the best; it's about actively engaging in the ongoing process of connecting with your partner on a level so deep that it weaves the fabric of a truly fulfilling life together.

Active Listening and Conflict Resolution

Active listening. It might sound like a fancy term from a psychology textbook, but it is something we all do (or should be doing) daily. It is a skill that can elevate your relationship from mundane to magical.

In our fast-paced lives, we often find ourselves more interested in speaking than in truly listening. We are so eager to get our point across or share our experiences that we often forget that listening is a two-way street. But the magic happens when we genuinely listen.

Active listening is not just about hearing words; it is about understanding the emotions, fears, and joys behind those words. It is about making your partner feel valued and heard. It is about being fully present in the moment.

The ABCS of Active Listening

How do you become an active listener? It's simpler than you think. Remember the ABCS:

A - Ask Open-Ended Questions: Instead of asking yes-or-no questions, ask questions that encourage your partner to open up. For instance, instead of asking, "Did you have a good day at work?" try "What was the highlight of your day?"

B - Be Present: Put away distractions. Turn off the TV, put down your phone, and focus on your partner. Give them your undivided attention.

C - Clarify and Reflect: If you are not sure you have understood correctly, ask for clarification. Reflect on what you have heard to ensure you got it right. This not only shows that you are listening but also helps your partner feel heard.

S - Show Empathy: Try to put yourself in your partner's shoes. Understand their feelings, even if you do not agree with them. Empathy bridges gaps and fosters connection.

Handling Conflict with Grace

Conflicts are a natural part of any relationship. But what sets successful couples apart is how they handle these conflicts. It is not about avoiding them but about addressing them with grace and respect.

Choose Your Battles: Not every issue requires a full-blown argument. Sometimes, it's best to let minor annoyances slide. Reserve your energy for the big stuff.

Stay Calm: When conflicts do arise, try to keep your emotions in check. Yelling and name-calling won't get you anywhere. Take a deep breath, and approach the conversation with a level head.

Use "I" Statements: Instead of pointing fingers and saying, "You always do this," express your feelings using "I" statements. For example, say, "I feel hurt when this happens."

Compromise: Successful conflict resolution often involves finding a middle ground. Be willing to meet your partner halfway and seek solutions together.

Seek Help If Needed: If you find yourselves stuck in a cycle of recurring conflicts, don't hesitate to seek help from a therapist or counsellor. They can provide valuable tools and guidance.

Developing Trust and Intimacy

Developing trust and intimacy is about nurturing a strong foundation of mutual reliability and emotional connection in your relationship. It involves open communication, vulnerability, and a deep understanding of each other's needs and desires. By fostering these elements, you can create an unshakeable bond and experience a profoundly intimate love.

Trust: The Foundation of Every Great Relationship

Trust is the bedrock upon which strong marriages are built. It is like a delicate plant that needs time, care, and attention to flourish.

Trust is built over time through consistent actions. If you say you will do something, do it. If you promise to be there, be there. Your words and actions should align.

Be honest with your partner, even when it's difficult. Lies and secrets erode trust faster than anything else. Trust that you can be vulnerable with each other.

Dependability is a key aspect of trust. Your partner should know they can count on you in times of need. Be their rock when life gets tough.

We are all human, and we all make mistakes. Forgiving your partner for their slip-ups, and seeking forgiveness when you err, is essential for rebuilding trust.

Intimacy: More Than Just Physical

Intimacy is often equated with physical closeness, but it is so much more than that. It is about being emotionally close, too.

Share your thoughts, feelings, and dreams with your partner. Let them into your inner world. Open, honest, and vulnerable conversations deepen intimacy.

Spend quality time together. Put away the distractions and create moments that are just for the two of you. It could be a simple dinner date or a weekend getaway. Physical intimacy is important, but it is not just about sex. Hugs, kisses, cuddles, and holding hands are all ways to express love and deepen your bond.

Intimacy thrives when you trust your partner enough to be your true self. Let your guard down and let them see the real you.

Building a deeper understanding of your partner is like discovering hidden treasure in your relationship. It is a journey that takes time and effort but is well worth it. Active listening and conflict resolution are the tools that keep communication flowing smoothly, while trust and intimacy are the bonds that make your connection unbreakable.

Your marriage is a living entity that needs nourishment and care. Keep practising these skills, and your relationship will not only survive but thrive. So, as you close this chapter, take a moment to reflect on how you can incorporate these principles into your marriage. And stay tuned for the next chapter, where we'll explore the power of shared goals and dreams in creating a fulfilling marriage. Until then, happy listening, resolving, trusting, and loving!

12

How Nature/ Nurture Impacts Relationships

"Nature and nurture conspire together. One must keep both in view. But, if we are interested in a full understanding of human behaviour, then nurture is especially important."

–Jesse J. Prinz

Contrary to what many believe, the foundation of a successful marriage is not just the coming together of 'singles' to start a marriage, it is the family. The family is the bedrock and foundation for the raising of a man or a female. There is a reason why the divine order established in Genesis was a family first then children came into the mix.

The family is the genesis of the raising of an individual.

If you are reading this, there is a 100% chance that you did not drop from the sky or grow out of the earth. You came from a family. The values, beliefs, and principles you uphold as an individual all came from the experiences and exposure you had while growing up.

The Impact of Nature/Nurture

Each of us bears natural traits and features that are a result of our race, genes, DNA, and other naturally occurring traits. All these form the 'nature' dimension of our being. You cannot change your height, shape, eyes, skeletal structure, etc. Why? These are naturally occurring; they are fitted to you from birth. There's little or nothing you can do to change that. On the other hand, there's nurture. This refers to the unique experiences, teachings, learning, values, and beliefs that have been passed down from a parent/guardians to their children.

This brings to mind the Iceberg Effect. When a lady or man is of marriageable age, what the world sees is simply the tip of the iceberg (for example their blossoming career, good looks, character flaws, struggles, low self-esteem, confidence, etc.) what is buried underneath that are years of conditioning and experiences that have shaped them into whom they have now become.

Many times, when singles are seeking partners, they are either carried away by the 'tip of the iceberg' of their desired suitors or distracted by it. There's more to a person than meets the eye. This is why this first chapter of the book is dedicated to understanding the 'nurture/nature' dimension of singleness.

Someone brought up in a first-world country, who attended an Ivy League School, and has travelled to more than 10 countries in the world would have a different worldview from another person of the same age (perhaps, even born the same day) living in a third world country in an environment of guns, drugs, and prostitutes and comes from a dysfunctional home.

That's what nurture does to us. Inherently, every human is the same. What makes us distinct is our nurture.

Take for example:

Shola grew up watching his parents working round the clock to make ends meet. He saw how his parents worked so hard to put food on the table and afford the best things of life yet loving him and his other siblings so much. He learned to appreciate hard work, family, and love. Even when he was away from home as a university student, he kept the image of his parents in his heart. He couldn't afford to make a mess of the opportunities they worked so hard to get him. He desired so much to make them proud and to be the best.

Sade, a colleague of Shola in the university, grew up in an environment where the least person drove at least 2 cars. Her parents were separated when she was 10 years old. Being the only child, her father gave her all she ever asked for in a bid to prove to his estranged wife that he could do a better job than she could ever do since he got custody of their child. Unknown to him, he was raising a girl who had no value for hard work and felt entitled wherever she found herself. Sade hardly took any tasks given to her seriously, she threw opportunities away like a bag of trash.

Now, looking at it from an observer's viewpoint, what do you see?

On the outside, people would desire to have the life of Sade or at least be her fiancé. Others could see Shola as another struggling student just because he doesn't have the flashy things that attract people. But underneath there are values and a lifetime of training and experiences that make him a more valuable person in the long run.

Now, imagine if Shola were to ask Sade to be his wife, what are the likely challenges they would face? They may appear cute together and have one or two similar interests, but compatibility and building a solid relationship may be a difficult task if both parties aren't willing to learn and change.

As singles, you cannot afford to take steps toward marriage with a person based on what you see in the now. You must dig deep, ask questions, and explore where the person is coming from. One of the characteristics that make God who He is, is not just his power and wisdom. It is his presence all through time. Our understanding of Him is not only tied to what He is doing and saying now but who He was and what He has said before now. The total of all these helps us understand His ways and walk with him. The same goes for us (his creation), we are a product of time and its experiences.

When people say 'we are wired differently' what they are saying is, we are nurtured differently.

For myself and my husband, we had peculiar upbringings and our experiences in life were peculiar. I was born and nurtured in a Muslim home till I found Christ. As the first child (and first daughter) I was naturally groomed to lead, care, nurture and be a role model. I found Christ much later before getting into the university. While I was an undergraduate, I began praying about my future husband. I desired certain traits. My preference was not only shaped by my own experiences but now, my faith in Christ.

How Can We Be Nurtured From Our Nature?

There are types of nurturing that must be understood here:

1. *Religious Nurturing:* Religious conditioning is powerful. Your faith colours your world. It is the lens through which you judge things. The way a Christian would judge a matter will be different from the way an atheist or a Buddhist would judge. The impact of your religious beliefs cannot be taken lightly. Being a marriage counsellor and a family-life practitioner has exposed me to the impact of religion on couples. Even couples of the same faith have serious challenges making critical decisions in the home due to the variance in the beliefs and doctrines they uphold. It cannot be neglected in the talking stage of would-be couples. For instance, some people believe a woman should only give birth naturally and that any other medically approved method such as C.S is demonic and should be resisted. Others do not want any form of piercing for their kids or want their daughters to wear trousers, etc. These issues may appear casual, but they bring up heated arguments within the home. This is why you cannot neglect the impact of one's faith in making a marital choice.

2. ***Social/Environmental Nurturing:*** This speaks to where an individual started life. Both parties need to understand the realities of one another. The environment plays a very critical role in our conditioning. If you had grown up in a different neighbourhood, there is a very high chance that you would have turned out differently and with a totally different set of beliefs and worldview.

3. ***Societal Nurturing:*** Moving from one society to another, affects nurturing too. There is an African society with its settings, mores, and norms; there is a European and American society, etc., all these have their way of impacting a person's upbringing. While many African countries clamp down on the rights of citizens (for example), in other developed nations, people can sue easily and can exercise their rights. So, such people are vocal and assertive about what they want. This kind of nurturing affects how such people see life even if they move to a different environment.

4. ***Cultural Nurturing:*** One's cultural background has a profound effect on our outlook on life. It affects our decisions and perspective. For example, a Yoruba elder would expect that a younger person prostrates or kneels to greet them. Whenever this is not done,

it attracts a frown or swift correction from the elder.

5. *Intellectual/Mental Nurturing:* where there is a willingness to pursue growth intellectually, there tends to be growth and maturity. Their level of knowledge and insight affects their social status. Interests are to be in sync to a large extent. It could lead to emotional affairs. An example of the lady who married a wealthy man but could not connect with him intellectually.

6. *Emotional Nurturing:* When parents express their love and affection to their children, they are nurturing them with positive emotions and when parents are abusive to their children and others, they are unconsciously conditioning them as well. Your capacity and that of your partner are tied to how they were groomed emotionally. Emotional nurturing is powerful, it affects how a person relates with other people.

13

The Negotiation Table

"A good marriage is one which allows for change and growth in the individuals and in the way they express their love."

– Pearl S. Buck

Relationships are like contracts and agreements which two people sign. In other words, if you want to succeed in your relationship, see it as a business.

The perfect demonstration of this happens when the couple gets together on the day of their wedding; they are whisked away from the crowd amidst the dance, rejoicing and fun-fare to sign a document that binds them together for life.

This should reveal to many singles, and even newly married, that they are not just in a relationship to exchange emotions and "fluids" but in a contract where certain terms and agreements are to be reached and adhered to.

In my many counselling sessions with premarital and post-marital couples, I evolved a concept which, for the first time, I will be making plain in this book, I call it the Negotiation Table.

Whenever companies are called to bid for large projects, they come with the regalia, portfolio and pomp to win the presentation and can become the ones to execute the projects. Couples must approach the relationship with the same mindset.

In this part of the world, everyone wants to get married believing that marriage is the end but the truth remains that marriage is just a means to the end. You can't just get married and relax. You keep working on either yourself, your spouse, your children, even your passion or your assignment hence marriage is not something you go into and have a sigh of relief. For the ladies, they feel like they've finally arrived, like they've landed in heaven and for the men, they have this feeling of accomplishment seeing that they've checked the box of marriage on their to-do list.

As previously stated, marriage can be likened to a business between two individuals. This means you cannot expect someone to go into business with you if you don't offer anything reasonable. You don't expect someone to go into business with you without first reviewing what you are bringing to the table. Even after the deal has been struck, each party is expected to keep up their end of the bargain else the business will crumble and fail.

The same goes for marriage; both partners are expected to do something so the marriage doesn't crumble and die. What you do to keep your marriage alive will have its roots on the negotiation table.

As stated by Dr. Olumide Emmanuel, "Marriage is a school where you don't graduate from which is why you obtain your certificate the day you enrol." This tells us, in essence, that marriage has just begun after the wedding day. You don't go into marriage feeling like you've arrived because you haven't, you just started the journey. Holding up your end of the bargain will come easy if you know what your bargain is to start with. What do you have to offer your spouse and marriage and what does your marriage have to offer God and your environment in return?

There must be something you're putting on the negotiation table of marriage. What are you exchanging, what are you bringing to the table?

VISION

The Bible says in Proverbs 29:18a *"Where there is no vision, the people perish..."*

Vision is an ideal or a goal toward which one aspires. A lot of relationships and marriages are perishing because they never defined their vision both personal and individual vision and collective or couple vision. Failure to define your visions means there's no destination and with no destination comes destruction. Even as a single being before considering marriage, it is strongly advised to have a vision for yourself. Know who you are and where you are going because even when the right person doesn't come when you expect, you are not desperate to fall into the hands of just anybody.

One of the things that helped me when I met my husband on campus, seeing I was never physically attracted to him, was that I had a glimpse of the direction I was heading towards and I knew what I wanted for my life. So even when the whole of my body was in total disagreement with him being my husband, my mind was constantly being drawn back to the vision I had of my husband. Yes, I had a vision of who my husband would be because I prayed about it. I did not start praying for and about my husband when we met but years before I even met him. My prayers were simple. I asked God for someone to complement me in areas of vision, assignment and passion. I asked God to give me a husband whose entire family are not just Christians but are born-again children of God. (This was important to me because of my background as a Muslim and as a young convert) and that he should be an engineer. These were the things among other things I asked God for. Even when I was saying NO, God reminded me of my prayers about the husband I wanted and how he is an answer to my prayers. If I did not have a list of what I wanted, I probably would have settled for anything.

Get whole also in the aspect of your vision not just because you need to get married but so you can fulfil your purpose and not just anybody in trousers will appeal to you. Remember this… "A guy may be good and fantastic in all other areas but if he's not in line with your vision and purpose, he automatically becomes a bad person for you." The same goes for the guys, if a good lady is not in line with your purpose, she is bad for you. It is important you know your vision and have a vision for your marriage before going into it.

IDENTITY

This is a very important aspect of an individual and has

to be discussed and understood by both parties before and even after tying the knot of marriage. You bring the wholeness of YOU to the table without holding anything back. Help your partner understand who you are and make efforts to do the same and if there are some sketchy parts of your identities, you could both work together to refine them. Take significant time to understand each other's temperaments. Find out, together, the dominant temperament(s) your spouse exhibits, study both their weaknesses and strengths and work on them together. Courtship is not the time for romance but a time to get to know as much as you can.

If you want your marriage to succeed, you're going to have to bring the whole of you and place it on the table.

One of the ingredients to having a successful marriage is LOVE and these four-lettered words have languages. In understanding your identities, you need to get a grasp on the languages of love. In simple terms, you need to understand what makes your spouse feel loved and also what makes you feel loved. You need to understand how best to speak love to your spouse and also how best you hear love. There are five love languages as written by Gary Chapman in his book, The Five Love Languages and I'll briefly talk about them.

The Language of Words of Affirmation.
This love language talks about how you constantly and deliberately speak positive, humble, kind, appreciative and encouraging words to your spouse.

The Language of Acts of Service
This works by simply lending a helping hand to your spouse, like carrying her bag or polishing his shoes, doing some home chores etc.

The Language of Receiving Gifts
Your partner feels loved the most when you give gifts no matter how little or big in value or worth.

The Language of Quality Time
Your partner feels loved more when you can spend quality and devoted time with them not minding how short or long it may seem.

The Language of Physical Touch
You speak this language by simply touching, like holding hands when you walk on the street, little pats on the back or little hugs here and there.

The love language you understand is the language you most likely speak and that might not be the language your partner understands and because they don't understand it, they can't speak it back to you. Your love language could be receiving gifts and that of your partner is quality time but because you feel loved by receiving gifts, you keep showering your partner with various kinds of gifts and they still don't feel loved because all they understand is quality time and if only, they could spend time with you, they would feel loved. To avoid all this drama of she/he loves me but doesn't show it, bring your whole identity to the table.

CHARACTER

We all have the good and the bad traits, the undeveloped and developed inborn. We cannot have characters that are similarly good or similarly bad in marriage. Although there is enough room for improvement, these characters, either good or bad, need to be put under check preferably by an external force. I will explain with a story about a friend.

She got married to a man who is emphatic to a fault. He could give away his life savings without even knowing it. He finds it very difficult to say NO to someone in need whereas his wife says NO without remorse. It is interesting to have both parties give like that but one of the disadvantages is that they would not achieve anything financially because they would have given everything out. The wife in this story serves as a check to her husband's giving. Coming to the negotiation table, you need to understand each other's strengths and weaknesses and be ready to evolve. Be open-minded. In terms of character, you are supposed to be like a round peg in your spouse's round hole and vice versa to complement each other. You can't both be round pegs or both round holes.

Using my marriage as an illustration. I am the first child and my husband is the first son and by this alone, we were going to have issues of control in my home. We both individually and separately had been controlling people before we got married. We both possess some level of leadership skills because of our positions in the family we came from so there is a tendency that I would have gone into marriage with my controlling nature and I'll begin to control and command my husband but I came to an understanding that only one person has to hold the steering wheel of a car for the car to safely get to its destination. You negotiate all these things before getting married.

FAMILY MAKEUP

Is there anything that could explode between the two families? Bring it up while negotiating. In my case, I came from a family that was at least doing well to survive with both parents and four younger siblings. When

I completed my university education, I went into the banking sector and this gave my parents some sort of relief that I was going to help take care of my younger siblings. It broke my parents' hearts when I told them about 2 years later that I was getting married. They were not happy that I was getting married early. We had to discuss it at the negotiation table. Will our marriage bring enmity between us and our families? Aside from that, you have to consider ways your extended families could affect the relationship with your immediate family.

Try to understand the family background of your spouse. Is he/she from a broken home or a polygamous home, is he/she an orphan, an only child, a first son, a firstborn or the breadwinner? Who are those that could interfere in your marriage? Talk about these things. I counselled a lady some time ago who was about to get married to an only child. The mother of her husband was already preparing a space in her house for them to live in after they got married. I just asked her if she's prepared for what is to come. Don't take these things for granted so you will not be a reactive couple in marriage but a proactive one.

VALUES

I define values as the intrinsic part of a person that cries out for expression and serves as a priority in his subconscious and conscious living. Some values are obvious and there are values we rarely take notice of. They are embedded in the deeper parts of a human, hence, I will advise couples to constantly communicate with each other. One other reason this is on the negotiation table is so you will not get into marriage and be taken aback by the value system of your spouse. These things need to be discussed before the wedding and even after.

There is a template of a value system I love working with "Mr. Fantastic" as written by Fela Durotoye. There are about seventeen value systems in this template which include FAMILY, FUN, FINANCE, FRIENDS, and others. The major way to know about people is to discuss it and you'll learn from both the words and the body language of the person involved. It is advisable to take advantage of every opportunity, even your hangouts and fun time, to ask questions because there are some questions you might have to re-ask. This singular act is not a show of distrust but for clarification and better understanding.

One other way to check out the value system of your spouse is to ask close family members and friends and also observe how they treat other people.

Before I said "Yes" to my husband, I had always seen

my husband helping other ladies because it made him uncomfortable to see ladies stressing or stressed. He always finds ways to help any lady he comes across. These things, for me, were pointers to how loving and caring he is.

After fully understanding the value system of your partner, you will have to prune it together with your partner. Find out the values you have in common and those that are peculiar. Find out the core values and those that are peripheral. Conclude with your partner about your value systems and this can be achieved with the process that has been explained earlier which I call the communication, Assimilation and Differentiation process. Note, while going through this process, avoid trying to change the whole value system of your partner because that is not the goal but to understand.

FRUIT OF THE SPIRIT

The fruit of the spirit can be narrowed down to character. These fruits as found in Galatians 5:22 & 23 (ERV) love, joy, peace, patience, kindness, goodness, faithfulness, gentleness and self-control can be seen in an individual's character and personality traits. The fruit of the spirit works in hand with the temperament of an individual.

My husband is short-fused even though he sometimes

seems to be reserved and I, on the other hand, could be a bit calmer-headed than him. On one of his business occasions, he was cheated on and extorted on a land lease he already paid for. The property owner decided not to let go of the land and at the same time isn't willing to refund. A meeting was called to resolve the issue but the landlord, for one reason or the other, rained hurtful words on my husband. I had to intervene so my husband would not have to say a word. Guess what I did… I went on my knees pleading with the man who cheated him and I pressed on my husband not to react because he was justifiably angry and he did not.

Now let's assume… Let's assume we were both short-fused, we would have turned that meeting into chaos and not be able to agree on anything but we understood how important it is to complement each other and also how to be patient: not reacting with the heat of the moment. After so much deliberation, an agreement was reached and the meeting was brought to a close but then just two weeks after the meeting, the property owner passed on. If my husband had responded according to his anger, what do you think would have been said about the arguments and my husband??

On another occasion, a couple came for counselling and the wife was on the verge of filing their divorce. The wife happened to be hot-tempered while the husband was on the cool end. She had a job and her husband didn't at the time which made her the breadwinner of the family. She was working far away from home so most nights she got back home and lashed out at her husband after having been stressed out by the long hours in traffic. For a woman like this, the absence of the right fruit of the spirit which is Patience, her marriage was going to suffer and as God may have it, they decided to come for counselling. To save the marriage, I had to puncture one of their value systems which had to do with pride of house ownership.

The couple lived in their house which made them landlords but the wife worked far from home while the husband was in ministry and also far from home. Mondays through to Fridays, the wife goes to work early and returns late, Saturdays could have been used for couple's bonding, the husband sets out in the morning for evangelism and also gets back home late and then on Sundays, they both go to church and return very exhausted. They never really had time to spend together. Their marriage lacked the bond which made their love slack and in turn, they could not tolerate each other anymore and they couldn't wait to end the marriage.

To create time for the couple, I advised that they get an apartment closer to the workplace and church which will result in spending more time with each other refreshed and not in traffic, exhausted. They did and their marriage is waxing strong because they spend more time together bonding, communicating and loving each other. Character and temperament are all under the fruit of the spirit.

Debunking Myths and Misconceptions about Marriage

"A great marriage is not when the 'perfect couple' comes together. It is when an imperfect couple learns to enjoy their differences."

—Dave Meurer

In our years as marriage counsellors, we have discovered some myths and misconceptions a lot of people have about marriage. These myths can sometimes shape your expectations and actions within your relationship, often leading to unnecessary stress and misunderstandings. By debunking these myths, we hope to shed light on what a successful marriage truly entails.

Misconception 1: The husband has to be the provider of money and material things.

One of the most persistent myths about marriage is

the idea that the husband must be the sole provider of financial support for the family. This misconception has deep historical roots, stemming from a time when traditional gender roles were more rigidly defined. However, in today's world, marriage is about partnership and shared responsibilities.

Reality:

In a healthy and fulfilling marriage, financial responsibilities are typically shared between both partners. Each person brings their unique skills, strengths, and contributions to the table. Whether it is through paid work, managing the household, or pursuing a joint entrepreneurial venture, the financial burden is a shared one. Embracing this partnership approach can lead to a more balanced and harmonious relationship.

Misconception 2: The way to a man's heart is through his stomach.

You have probably heard the saying, "The way to a man's heart is through his stomach." While there is no denying that good food can bring joy to a relationship, this myth oversimplifies the complexities of romantic bonds.

Reality:

Love and emotional connection in a marriage go far

beyond culinary skills. However, circumstances could call for a role switch for the health, peace, and progress of that family, as no two marriages are the same. A husband who is a chef or cook will be better than his wife in terms of cooking. What is important is to avoid taking advantage of each other and be mutually understanding and intentional. The wife ensures she gets better in her areas of weakness when it comes to her responsibilities, while the husband supports her. No two marriages are the same.

Misconception 3: The place of the woman is the kitchen.
This myth suggests that a woman's primary role within a marriage is limited to cooking and taking care of the household. Such stereotypes can be limiting and unfair to both partners.

Reality:
The traditional role of caring for the home and managing domestic activities and childcare is emphasized by the wife. However, in modern marriages, partners need to be more flexible and understanding in order to keep the family intact and strong in bond. While both partners have freedom to pursue their dreams and goals, it must not be at the detriment of the marriage and family.

Misconception 4: Marriage will solve all your problems.
Some people believe that getting married will magically resolve all of their personal issues and make life perfect. This myth can lead to unrealistic expectations and disappointment.

Reality:

Marriage is not a panacea for life's challenges. In fact, it can sometimes magnify pre-existing issues. A healthy and fulfilling marriage is built on a foundation of two individuals who are already content and self-aware. It is crucial to address personal issues and growth independently before seeking fulfillment through marriage. A strong partnership can support personal growth, but it cannot replace it.

Misconception 5: Love is enough to sustain a marriage
While love is undoubtedly a crucial ingredient in a successful marriage, it is not the only one. This myth oversimplifies the complexities of a long-term relationship.

Reality:

Love is the starting point, but it must be accompanied by commitment, communication, trust, and effort. A lasting marriage requires ongoing work from both partners to maintain and strengthen the bond. Love alone cannot overcome challenges or sustain a marriage through difficult times. It is essential to nurture all aspects of your relationship to ensure its longevity.

Misconception 6: Once you are married, you should always put your spouse first.

While prioritizing your spouse is essential, this myth can lead to neglecting your own needs and well-being, which can ultimately harm the relationship.

Reality:

A successful marriage is a balance between prioritizing your spouse and taking care of yourself. It is essential to maintain a healthy sense of self and pursue individual interests and passions. A strong marriage is built on two individuals who are fulfilled and happy independently, coming together to enhance each other's lives. Finding this balance is key to a lasting and fulfilling marriage.

Misconception 7: Marriage should be effortless.

Some people believe that if they have found the right person, everything in their marriage should come easily and without effort. This myth can lead to frustration and disappointment when challenges inevitably arise.

Reality:

Marriage requires effort, patience, and a willingness to work through difficulties. It is entirely normal to face obstacles and conflicts within a marriage. What distinguishes successful marriages is the ability to confront and resolve these challenges together, growing stronger in the process. Effort invested in maintaining and nurturing your relationship is a sign of commitment and love.

Misconception 8: Once you have children, your marriage will be complete.
While children can bring joy and fulfillment to a marriage, they also introduce new complexities and demands.

Reality:

Children are a significant part of many marriages, but they should not be seen as the sole purpose or completion of a marriage. A successful marriage involves a balance between the roles of partners as spouses and parents. It is essential to maintain the romantic and emotional connection with your spouse even as you embrace your roles as parents. Nurturing your relationship allows you to provide a stable and loving environment for your children.

Misconception 9: Marriage should always be passionate and exciting.

The idea that marriage should always be filled with passion and excitement can lead to unrealistic expectations and disappointment when everyday life sets in.

Reality:

Passion and excitement are essential ingredients in a fulfilling marriage, but they may ebb and flow over time. What replaces them is a deeper sense of intimacy and companionship that can be equally, if not more, satisfying. A strong marriage is built on a foundation of love, trust, and shared experiences that go beyond the initial honeymoon phase.

Misconception 10: You can change your spouse.

Many people enter into marriage hoping to change certain aspects of their partner's personality or behavior. This myth can lead to frustration and resentment.

Reality:

It is crucial to accept your partner for who they are and not try to change them. While personal growth and self-improvement are essential, trying to fundamentally change your spouse rarely leads to positive outcomes. Instead, focus on open and honest communication, compromise, and finding ways to work together to address any issues or differences.

Debunking these common misconceptions about marriage is a crucial step in building a strong and fulfilling partnership. A successful marriage is not about conforming to outdated stereotypes or unrealistic expectations. It is about creating a partnership based on mutual respect, open communication, and shared values.

PART FOUR

APPLICATION

15

Decision Making

"A perfect marriage is just two imperfect people who refuse to give up on each other."

—Unknown

There were five black birds sitting on a tree. They all decided to fly away. How many birds are left? How many times have you made decisions in your life and not followed through with action? We have all been there. We decide to eat healthier, but we keep reaching for that bag of chips. We decide to start exercising, but our sneakers gather dust in the closet. We decide to improve our relationships, but we continue with the same old habits.

Now, back to those five birds. If you are like most people, you probably thought that once they decided to fly away, there would be no birds left on the tree. But the truth is, the answer is "Five." Why? Because the birds decided, but they did not take action. They remained on the tree.

Decisions alone don't change anything. It is the action that transforms your life, just as applying what you learn can transform your relationship. The RICA Model is not just about understanding; it is about doing.

Are you a decider or a doer in your relationship?

Many couples fall into the trap of making grand decisions without following through. They decide to communicate better, spend more quality time together, or resolve conflicts peacefully, but when it comes to implementation, they fall short. The result? Frustration and unfulfilled promises.

To achieve a fulfilling marriage, it is crucial to transition from being a mere decider to becoming a proactive doer. It is time to bridge the gap between intention and action.

Remember, change does not happen overnight. Just like those birds on the tree, it may take time before you see the fruits of your actions. But if you persist and stay committed, you will gradually transform your marriage or relationship into a fulfilling and harmonious partnership.

As we move forward, always keep in mind the lesson of the five birds. Decisions are essential, but they are only the beginning. The real power lies in taking action. Apply what you have learned, and watch your marriage thrive. It is time to become a doer, not just a decider.

In the words of Proverbs 24:3-4 (NIV), *"By wisdom, a house is built, and through understanding, it is established; through knowledge, its rooms are filled with rare and beautiful treasures."*

Strengthening Your Emotional Connections

"Happy is the man who finds a true friend, and far happier is he who finds that true friend in his wife."

—Franz Schubert

In the beginning, love often feels effortless. It is like sailing on calm seas with the wind at your back. But as the years go by, maintaining that emotional connection becomes increasingly important. Here is how the RICA Model can help you strengthen your emotional bond:

Recognizing Emotions:

The first step in nurturing your emotional connection is recognizing and acknowledging your own emotions and those of your partner. It is easy to brush feelings aside in the hustle and bustle of life, but doing so can lead to emotional disconnection. Take time to check in with yourself and your partner regularly. Ask, "How are you feeling today?" and be open to sharing your own emotions as well.

Investing Time in Communication:
Communication is the lifeblood of any relationship. The RICA Model encourages open and honest conversations. Do not just talk about your day; discuss your hopes, dreams, and fears. Share your aspirations and actively listen to your partner's thoughts and feelings. Effective communication builds trust and deepens your emotional connection.

Cultivating Empathy:
Empathy is the ability to understand and share the feelings of another. It is a cornerstone of a strong emotional connection. Put yourself in your partner's shoes and try to see the world from their perspective. This not only fosters understanding but also shows that you care deeply about their feelings.

Appreciating Small Moments:
Often, it is the small, everyday moments that contribute most to a strong emotional connection. Take time to appreciate these moments, whether it is a shared laugh, a comforting hug, or a quiet evening together. These

seemingly insignificant moments can strengthen your bond over time.

Navigating Common Challenges in Marriage

Marriage is not all sunshine and rainbows; it comes with its fair share of storms. Common challenges, such as finances, parenting, and career, can test your relationship.

Respecting Individuality:
One of the biggest challenges in a marriage is balancing individuality with togetherness. Respect each other's unique needs and goals. Understand that both partners can pursue personal growth and fulfilment while still being committed to the relationship.

Inclusive Decision-Making:
Financial decisions, parenting choices, and career moves often require joint decisions. Sit down together, discuss your options, and find solutions that work for both of you. When both partners have a say in major decisions, it fosters a sense of partnership and shared responsibility.

Compromise, Not Sacrifice:
Marriage requires compromise, but it is essential to differentiate between compromise and sacrifice. Compromise means finding solutions that meet

both partners' needs, while sacrifice implies giving up something essential for the sake of the relationship. Strive for compromise, and when necessary, seek professional help to find solutions that respect both individuals.

Adapting to Change:

Life is constantly changing, and so are the challenges you face as a couple. When life throws curveballs, approach them as a team. Embrace change together, supporting each other through the ups and downs.

Maintaining a Blissful Marriage Over Time

The final leg of our journey explores how to maintain a blissful marriage over time. It's not just about surviving; it's about thriving together. The RICA Model offers valuable insights:

Rekindling Romance:

As the years go by, it's easy to let romance take a back seat. Maintaining a blissful marriage requires intentional effort. Plan date nights, surprise each other with gestures of love, and never stop saying "I love you." Keeping the romance alive can reignite the spark in your relationship.

Investing in Self-Care:

A happy marriage begins with happy individuals. Self-care is not selfish; it is an essential part of maintaining a strong partnership. Prioritise self-care routines that rejuvenate you, physically and emotionally. When both partners are fulfilled and content individually, it positively impacts the marriage.

Celebrate Milestones:

Do not wait for anniversaries to celebrate your relationship. Celebrate even the smallest milestones – the day you met, your first home, or a significant achievement. These celebrations create a sense of joy and appreciation for the journey you've shared.

Always Learning:

A blissful marriage is a dynamic one. You must keep learning. Read books, attend workshops, or seek counselling when needed. Commit to being lifelong students of love and partnership.

Remember, every marriage is unique, and there's no one-size-fits-all solution. The RICA Model is a flexible guide, allowing you to tailor it to your specific circumstances. Whether you are just starting your marital adventure or you are a seasoned traveller, the principles within these pages can help you build and maintain a fulfilling and joyful partnership.

With dedication and commitment, you can create a marriage that not only withstands the test of time but thrives in its embrace.

The Journey Ahead

"A good marriage is one which allows for change and growth in the individuals and in the way they express their love."

—Pearl S. Buck

Marriage is a journey, not a destination. It is a path filled with twists and turns, challenges and triumphs, and a constant evolution of both individuals and the relationship itself. The moment you say "I do," you embark on a lifelong adventure, one that has the potential to bring immense joy and fulfilment. But like any journey, it requires a roadmap, a sense of direction, and the willingness to adapt along the way.

The Ongoing Process of Growth and Transformation in Marriage

When you think of marriage, what comes to mind? Perhaps you envision a romantic wedding, a loving partnership, or a lifelong commitment. While all of these are integral parts of marriage, they represent just a snapshot of a much larger picture. Marriage is not static; it is a dynamic entity that requires ongoing effort and nurturing.

Imagine your marriage as a garden. Just like a garden needs constant care, attention, and occasional pruning, so does your relationship. If you neglect it, the weeds of miscommunication, neglect, and complacency can quickly take over. But if you tend to it with love, respect, and intention, your marriage can blossom into something truly beautiful.

Here are some key aspects of the ongoing growth and transformation in marriage:

1. **Setting Goals and Aspirations:** To grow as individuals and as a couple, it is important to set goals and aspirations for your marriage. These goals can be big or small, short-term or long-term, but they should reflect what you both want to achieve together. Whether it is improving communication, deepening intimacy, or pursuing shared interests, having a clear vision for your marriage provides direction and purpose.

2. **Embracing Change:** Change is inevitable in life and

marriage. It could be a change in circumstances, such as a job relocation or the birth of a child, or it could be personal growth and development. Embracing change means being open to new experiences, challenges, and opportunities as a couple. It is about adapting together and supporting each other through life's transitions.

3. **Continuous Learning:** Just as you would not expect to become an expert in a field without ongoing education, you can not expect your marriage to thrive without continuous learning. This includes learning about your partner's needs, preferences, and evolving desires. It also involves learning new ways to communicate effectively and resolve conflicts constructively.

4. **Prioritising Quality Time**: In the hustle and bustle of daily life, it is easy to let quality time with your spouse fall by the wayside. However, spending meaningful, quality time together is essential for maintaining emotional intimacy. Whether it is a weekly date night, a weekend getaway, or simply enjoying a quiet evening at home, prioritise moments of connection.

5. **Seeking Support and Guidance:** No marriage is without its challenges, and seeking support when needed is a sign of strength, not weakness. This can come in the

form of marriage counselling, reading self-help books, or attending workshops and seminars. Don't hesitate to reach out for help when facing difficult issues.

6. **Celebrating Milestones:** Celebrate your achievements as a couple, both big and small. Milestones can include anniversaries, personal accomplishments, or even overcoming obstacles together. Celebrations remind you of the progress you have made and reinforce your commitment to each other.

7. **Maintaining Individuality:** While marriage is about partnership, it is also important to maintain your individuality. Pursuing your interests, hobbies, and personal growth not only enriches your own life but also adds depth and diversity to your relationship.

8. **Practising Forgiveness:** Mistakes and misunderstandings are inevitable, but forgiveness is a choice. Practice forgiveness in your marriage, letting go of grudges and resentment. It is a powerful way to promote healing and move forward together.

Resources for Further Support and Education

Embarking on the journey of strengthening your marriage is a commendable and worthwhile endeavour. While this book will provide you with valuable insights and strategies, there are many other resources available to support and enhance your efforts. Whether you're looking for expert advice, additional reading materials, or opportunities for personal growth, the following resources can be valuable companions on your marital journey:

Marriage Counselling

Marriage counsellors are trained professionals who can provide guidance and support for couples facing challenges in their relationships. They offer a safe and neutral space for open communication, conflict resolution, and personal growth. Consider seeking the services of a licensed marriage counsellor if you and your partner are struggling to navigate issues in your marriage.

Books on Marriage and Relationships

There is a wealth of literature on marriage and relationships, ranging from classic works to contemporary bestsellers. These books cover a wide range of topics, including communication, intimacy, conflict resolution, and personal development. Some notable authors in this genre include Gary Chapman, Kingsley Okonkwo, Mildred Okonkwo, John Gottman, Sue Johnson, and Esther Perel. Explore these books to gain deeper insights into the complexities of marriage.

Workshops and Seminars

Many organisations and institutions offer workshops and seminars focused on enhancing marital relationships. These events often provide practical tools and exercises to improve communication, strengthen emotional bonds, and resolve conflicts constructively. Look for local or online workshops that align with your needs and interests.

Online Resources and Communities

The internet is a treasure trove of resources for couples seeking support and education. Numerous websites, forums, and social media groups are dedicated to marriage and relationship advice. These platforms allow you to connect with other couples facing similar challenges, share experiences, and learn from a diverse range of perspectives.

Podcasts and Webinars

Podcasts and webinars offer convenient ways to access expert advice and insights on marriage and relationships. Many relationship experts host podcasts where they discuss various aspects of partnership, communication, and personal growth. Consider subscribing to relevant podcasts or attending webinars that resonate with you.

Retreats and Getaways

Marriage retreats and getaways provide couples with an opportunity to disconnect from their daily routines and focus on their relationship. These experiences often combine therapeutic workshops with relaxation and recreation. Whether it is a weekend retreat or an extended vacation, these immersive experiences can rejuvenate your marriage.

Support Groups

Support groups bring together individuals and couples facing similar challenges, such as infertility, addiction recovery, or grief. Joining a support group can provide a sense of community and shared understanding. It can also be a valuable source of emotional support and practical advice.

Trusted Friends and Family

Don't underestimate the power of your social circle. Trusted friends and family members can offer valuable insights, a listening ear, and a different perspective on your relationship. Sometimes, talking to someone who knows you well can provide clarity and support.

Continuing Education

Consider enrolling in courses or workshops related to personal development, communication skills, or emotional intelligence. These skills can have a profound impact on your marriage. Many educational institutions and online platforms offer courses in these areas.

Remember that every marriage is unique, and what works for one couple may not work for another. Explore these resources with an open mind, and do not hesitate to seek support when needed. Your commitment to strengthening your marriage through ongoing learning and growth is a testament to your love and dedication to each other.

What Type Of Couple Are You?

"A happy marriage is the union of two good forgivers."

—Ruth Bell Graham

In my journey as a marriage counsellor, I have come across several couples; each having their own uniqueness. I have been able to categorize couples into these four broad categories.

IGNORANT COUPLES IN MARRIAGE

An ignorant spouse is one who errs unintentionally but is willing to make amends the moment he or she attains the level of self-awareness regarding certain issues. It isthe beginning of deliverance from self-sabotaging behavioral patterns that kill marital relationships.

Pastor Lola and his wife, Lara (not their real names) came for a counseling session. It became clear to them that after six years of marriage, there was no improvement in all spheres of their lives. Lara stared at me during the counselling session and retorted "Since we got married, nothing has changed positively for us due to my husband's cultural attitude and his inability to carry out some domestic chores as a means of relief. I have told him that we shall remain stagnant in life if he doesn't change."

Her words were like a major blow to me because I wondered how Lara chose to be stagnant. After series of counselling sessions, they came to understand what they needed to do. They are doing very well today.

Azuka was introduced to me by her close friend, Tara (not their real names). It was a time when Azuka had totally written off her marriage. She had gone ahead to rent an apartment very close to her office. She was about to commence filing for divorce. It appeared to her that there was no hope, so much so that her siblings even gathered to beat her husband in one of their regular misunderstandings.

We discovered that in the process of counselling, we were able to reveal her blind spots to her. She never knew she was partly the cause of their marital issues. We met again two years after her counselling sessions, she openly told everyone at a function about how attending our counselling classes changed her marriage from a gloomy to a great marriage.

Job 36:12: But if they do not listen, they perish by the sword and die without knowledge.

ARROGANTLY IGNORANT COUPLES IN MARRIAGE

These are spouses that do not have the knowledge and are too proud to accept the fact that they are ignorant.

Phebian had been married to Roseline (not their real names) for 11years. He claimed Roselyn deceived him into marrying her due to his health. For the first 5 years of their marriage, it was a daily fight between them. Until I met them. In spite of several counselling sessions, Phebian never accepted that he had his own weaknesses such as anger, and domineering nature. I called it quit with them because he became an unwilling client. I had realized that there is nothing the best of counsellors can achieve with an unwilling client. Phebian recently filed for divorce after 11 years of unrealistic expectations from his spouse.

ARROGANT COUPLES IN MARRIAGE

An arrogant spouse is one who is too proud to seek help even when it is obvious, he or she needs help.

I once counseled a couple online who have been married for six years. I had to consent to counsel them even though the husband had shown some reasonable level of pride. I did that because of a mutual friend who referred the wife to me. He speaks on the phone as if he was always doing me a favor by attending the online counselling. Of course, the result has been very slow and he still complains that his wife Bisola can't change. He is so oblivious of the fact that the major change should come from him for their marriage to work.

INTENTIONAL SPOUSE

These are spouses who are always willing to work in their marriages as if their entire lives depend on it. Marriage is truly the fulfilment of Destiny and purpose hence in an ideal home, the couple should gravitate toward becoming an intentional couple.

Philippians 4:13, "I can do all things through Christ who strengthens me.: We have the capacity to be intentional if we want to.

One of the most remarkable counselling experiences we had was the one for Mr. & Mrs. Ayo Craig. Two weeks into their marriage, it appeared the marriage would be called off due to some irreconcilable differences. With persistence and clarity of vision and values and through prayers, they are waxing stronger together. It's been four years into their marriage. They are so quick to refer intending couples to us for counselling. They became more aware and more intentional about doing marriage right.

19

The Enduring Benefits of a Fulfilling Marriage

"A successful marriage requires falling in love many times, always with the same person."

—Mignon McLaughlin

Imagine a stone being thrown into a calm pond. The initial splash creates ripples that spread outwards, affecting the entire surface of the water. Similarly, a blissful marriage creates a ripple effect that touches not only the lives of the couple but also their families, friends, and communities. Let's delve into the lasting benefits of such a union.

- *Emotional Well-being:* A blissful marriage is a source of emotional support and security. When two people feel loved, valued, and understood, they are better equipped to handle life's challenges. This emotional well-being extends to the couple's children, who grow up in a nurturing environment, learning the importance of healthy relationships.

- *Physical Health:* Numerous studies have shown that married individuals tend to enjoy better physical health. A happy marriage can reduce stress, boost the immune system, and even increase longevity. This is not to say that marriage is a panacea, but rather that a supportive and loving partnership can have a positive impact on your well-being.

- *Mental Health:* The emotional connection in a blissful marriage can also contribute to better mental health. Partners in such marriages often report lower levels of anxiety and depression. Having someone to confide in and share life's ups and downs with can be a powerful antidote to the challenges of modern life.

- *Financial Stability:* In a loving partnership, couples often work together to achieve common financial goals. Whether it is budgeting, saving, or investing, a unified approach to finances can lead to greater financial stability and security.

- *Social Connections:* Happy couples tend to have strong social networks. They are more likely to engage with others, host gatherings, and be active in their communities. This not only enriches their own lives but also positively impacts the people around them.

- *Parenting Success:* For those who choose to have children, a blissful marriage provides a solid foundation for effective co-parenting. Children raised in such an environment often develop strong emotional intelligence and healthy relationship skills.

- *Fulfilment and Happiness*: Ultimately, the enduring benefit of a blissful marriage is the sense of fulfilment and happiness it brings. When you have a partner who loves and supports you, life becomes more meaningful and enjoyable. You have a companion to share your dreams, successes, and even the occasional failures.

Encouragement to Continue Applying the RICA Model Principles

After exploring the long-lasting advantages of a blissful marriage, it is essential to remember that maintaining such a relationship requires ongoing effort and commitment. The RICA model provides a framework that can guide you through the journey of marriage, helping you build and sustain the love and connection you desire.

1. *Reflect:* Continue to reflect on your actions and feelings. Self-awareness is a crucial component of a successful marriage. Understand your own needs, desires, and triggers, and be willing to communicate them openly with your partner.

2. *Invest*: Just as you invest in your financial future, invest time and effort in your relationship. Make a conscious effort to nurture your connection through quality time, thoughtful gestures, and acts of love and kindness.

3. *Communicate:* Effective communication is the lifeblood of any relationship. Keep the lines of communication open and honest. Be an active listener and practice empathy when your partner shares their thoughts and feelings.

4. *Adapt:* Life is constantly changing, and so are you and

your partner. Be willing to adapt and grow together. Be open to new experiences and challenges, and see them as opportunities for growth rather than obstacles.

5. *Seek Help When Needed:* There is no shame in seeking professional help if you encounter significant challenges in your marriage. A qualified therapist or counsellor can provide valuable guidance and tools to help you navigate difficult times.

6. *Celebrate Your Successes:* Take time to celebrate the small and big successes in your marriage. Acknowledge the progress you've made and the love you continue to share. Celebrate anniversaries, milestones, and everyday moments of joy.

7. *Be Patient:* Building a lasting and fulfilling marriage takes time. There will be ups and downs, but remember that the journey itself is a valuable part of your shared experience. Be patient with yourself and your partner as you both strive to be the best versions of yourselves.

Final Thoughts on the Journey to a Fulfilling and Lasting Partnership

As we conclude our exploration of "The RICA Model: The Pathway to a Fulfilling Marriage," it is important to recognize that a successful marriage is not a destination but a lifelong journey. It is a journey filled with learning, growth, and the deepening of your connection with your partner.

Remember that every marriage is unique, and there is no one-size-fits-all solution. The RICA model is a guide, but you have the flexibility to adapt it to your specific circumstances and needs. Your love story is yours to write, and you have the power to shape it into a beautiful and enduring narrative.

Reflect on the words of the famous poet, Rumi: *"Let yourself be silently drawn by the strange pull of what you love. It will not lead you astray."*

In the pursuit of a fulfilling and lasting partnership, let love be your guiding force. Let it lead you through the joys and challenges of marriage, and may your journey be filled with happiness, connection, and a deep sense of fulfilment.

Appendix:
Know Your Personality Types

With the RICA Model as our compass, let us set sail into the fascinating world of personality types within marriage.

THE PASSANGER PLANE – (SANGUINE)

THE PEOPLE PERSONALITY

The Passenger Plane (Sanguine)

Just like the features of the Passenger Plane, they are classy, fashion-conscious, and love brands. The way the plane accommodates first-class, business-class, and economy passengers and makes everyone feel great is the way passengers' personalities relate to each other.

These individuals are friendly, great relators, and fantastic communicators; they respond well to changes. However, they need to work on their impulsive nature; they could be disorganised and forgetful; they are likely to exaggerate whenever they talk; they are prone to talking more than action, just like the Apostle Peter in the Bible.

As it relates to relationships and marriage, they are prone to having flirtatious tendencies as a result of their body gestures. They love to relate to people through touch (hugs, handshakes, pecking, etc.). That sometimes puts them in trouble because their expressions are often misinterpreted.

If you are married to someone of this personality, please create an opportunity for him or her to express themselves; never accuse them of lying, even though they are the most prone to that due to the fact that they always want to be convincing. Make them vulnerable to you because it will help you both overcome any emotional affairs that may want to set in.

Do you also know that they have the most emotional and least disciplined personalities? The contrast of this should be intentionally and prayerfully monitored and overcome.

THE FIGHTER JET – (CHOLERIC)

THE PURPOSE PERSONALITY

The Fighter Jet (Choleric)

When you imagine or view these aircraft, they are built for war or challenges. There is no room for frivolities. Speed and the ability to weather challenging situations are their unique points.

These individuals are bold, assertive, and always ready for action. Fighter Jets in a marriage are like high-speed roller coasters. They are workaholics and can inject a burst of energy into your life. They thrive on challenges and are often natural leaders. However, they can be prone to anger and may need to work on their patience. They are also low in people management and communication skills.

If you are in a relationship with a Fighter Jet, producing results or evidence is key rather than arguing with them. They are also not as emotional as other personalities. Tears or stories rarely move them as much as you produce results or solutions to their expectations of you.

They appreciate directness and value partners who can keep up with their pace. Mutual respect is vital to ensuring a balanced partnership.

THE CARGO PLANE- (PHLEGMATIC)

THE PLEASANT PERSONALITY

3. The Cargo Plane (Phlegmatic)

The Cargo Plane is built to carry the heavy load or luggage of people. This is so apt for personalities like this, as they often sacrifice for others much more than themselves.

Cargo Planes are intelligent, steady, team-spirited, and great listeners and excel at handling responsibilities they have mastered for years.

They are the ones who ensure everything runs smoothly behind the scenes.

Cargo Planes provide stability and security in a relationship. They are responsible and often love to handle household duties and finances. However, they may need encouragement to open up emotionally and embrace spontaneity.

In a marriage with a Cargo Plane, it is important to acknowledge their contributions and express gratitude. Communication should focus on sharing responsibilities and finding ways to infuse more excitement into your life together. They do not thrive where they are shouted at, rushed, or forced to do things.

THE PRIVATE JET - Melancholy

4. The Private Jets (Melancholy)

The Private Jet as the name implies, is custom-built to accommodate a few passengers. This is so true of a Private Jet personality. They thrive better with a few friends than with lots of people. The personalities are perfectionists by nature. They are analytical in nature. They love to cross their Ts and dot their I's.

They are practical, grounded, and excel at handling responsibilities. They are the ones who ensure everything runs smoothly behind the scenes.

Private Jets are faithful, loyal, responsible, and often handle household duties and finances. However, they may need encouragement to open up emotionally and embrace spontaneity.

In a marriage with a Private Jet, it is important to strive hard to execute your goals or mutual agreement to the letter. Be time-conscious and validate integrity. Don't trigger surprises or fun without fully understanding their little and limited priorities for fun and fantasies.

However, they may need encouragement to step out and take risks.

Develop Self Awareness through the Johani Window

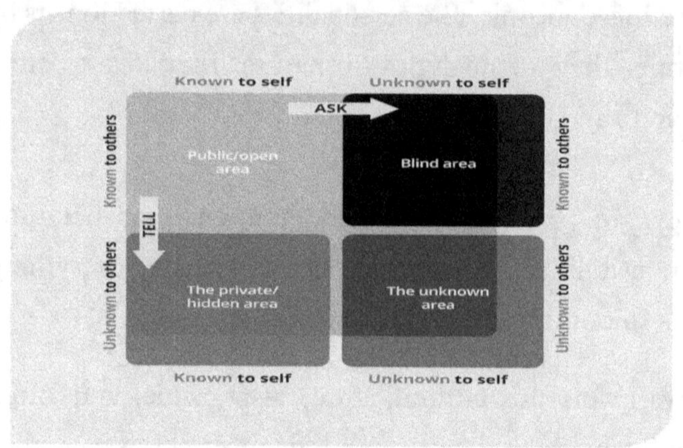

The Johari Window is a psychological tool and model used to help individuals understand their interpersonal communication and relationships. It was developed by psychologists Joseph Luft and Harry Ingham in 1955, combining their first names to create the term "Johari."

Simply put, the Johari Window is a tool that helps people understand themselves and how they communicate with others. The Johari Window consists of a four-quadrant grid that represents different aspects of our personality and self-awareness. They are:

Open Area (Arena): Things about you that you and others know. It's like the stuff you share openly. It includes behaviors, feelings, thoughts, and experiences that are openly shared and understood by both the individual and those around them.

Blind Area (Blind Spot): Things about you that others see, but you don't. It's like when people notice something about you that you didn't realise. It includes information or traits that others see in the individual but of which the individual is unaware. Feedback and communication from others can help reduce this blind spot.

Hidden Area (Facade): Things about you that you know but keep hidden from others. It's like your secret thoughts and feelings. These may include private thoughts, feelings, or experiences that the individual chooses not to disclose. Over time, trust and self-disclosure can expand the open area.

Unknown Area: Things about you that nobody knows yet. It's like undiscovered parts of yourself. It includes undiscovered or subconscious aspects of a person's personality that may emerge through self-discovery, personal growth, or therapy.

The Johari Window is often used in self-awareness exercises, group therapy, and interpersonal communication training to improve self-understanding, enhance relationships, and increase awareness of how one's behavior and thoughts impact others. The goal is to expand the open area, reduce the blind and hidden areas, and facilitate personal growth and effective communication.

Do this by circling as many traits that describe you and also asking those closest to you to circle out characteristics that describe you. After ward, include it in your Johani Window Open Area:

able	accepting	adaptable	bold	brave	calm	caring
cheerful	clever	complex	confident	dependable	dignified	energetic
extroverted	friendly	giving	happy	helpful	idealistic	independent
ingenious	intelligent	introverted	kind	knowledgeable	logical	loving
mature	modest	nervous	observant	organized	patient	powerful
proud	quiet	reflective	relaxed	religious	responsive	searching
self-assertive	self-conscious	sensible	sentimental	shy	silly	spontaneous
sympathetic	tense	trustworthy	warm	wise	witty	

About the authors

Sola & Nike Ajayi are Certified Family Life Practitioners, Pastors, and and thriving Entrepreneurs. With a wealth of experience and a deep commitment to guiding and nurturing relationships, they stand as pillars of wisdom and support.

Ministry Leadership

Dedicating themselves to spiritual leadership, the couple serves as Pastors responsible for the RCCG Sunshine Assembly Zone. Additionally, they assume the role of coordinating Pastors for the Young Adults and Youth at RCCG, Lagos Province 7. Their leadership extends beyond the spiritual realm as they have ventured into various other areas.

Professional Training and Accreditation

Sola & Nike Ajayi's expertise in Family Life Coaching and Marriage Counseling is a result of rigorous training and accreditation from prestigious institutions. They have been certified by The Institute of Family Engineering & Development in Nigeria, The Rising Oaks Ministry in Canada, The Institute of Marriage and Family Affairs in the USA, and the RCCG National Family Affairs Unit.

Realm Academy for Family Life

As visionaries behind the REALM ACADEMY FOR FAMILY LIFE, Sola & Nike Ajayi have established a comprehensive platform to cater to diverse aspects of family development. This innovative academy is home to six distinctive groups:

- *Relationship and Marriage Mentors Program:* Offering guidance to couples at every stage of their relationship journey.
- *Personal Progress Program:* Empowering individuals with personal growth tools and strategies.
- *Get Set... Marry:* Providing expert insights for singles on the path to marriage.
- *The Marriage Match Minder:* Assisting couples in building strong and lasting marriages.
- *Cradle ⅖:* Catering to parents in nurturing and raising children.
- *Happily Ever After:* Focusing on sustaining joyful and fulfilling marriages.

Personal Journey

With nearly two decades of marriage, Sola & Nike Ajayi are living examples of the principles they teach. Their union is blessed with three remarkable children who are destined to make a positive impact on the world.

Sola & Nike Ajayi's dedication to fostering healthy relationships, their diverse expertise, and their dynamic leadership have positioned them as significant influencers in the realm of family life and marriage coaching.

Other books written by Sola & Nike Ajayi include:

- Get Set, Marry
- Counselling Made Simple
- The ABC of Intentional Sex in Marriage